STILL DANCING

Still Dancing

Poems

Mary Thomson

RED SQUIRREL PRESS

First published in 2023 by Red Squirrel Press
36 Elphinstone Crescent
Biggar
South Lanarkshire
ML12 6GU
www.redsquirrelpress.com

Edited by Elizabeth Rimmer

Layout, design and typesetting by Gerry Cambridge
e: gerry.cambridge@btinternet.com

Cover images: Silhouette of couple: © LaInspiratriz/shutterstock.com
Old woman with Dog: © majivecka/shutterstock.com

A CIP catalogue record for this book is available from
the British Library.

ISBN: 978 1 913632 55 7

Red Squirrel Press is committed to a sustainable future.
This publication is printed in the UK by Imprint Digital
using Forest Stewardship Council certificated paper.
www.digital.imprint.co.uk

Contents

'The one most important thing I have learned over the years is the difference between taking one's work seriously and taking one's self seriously. The first is imperative and the second is disastrous.'

Margot Fonteyn, dancer:
quoted in *Simpson's Contemporary Quotations* (1988)

My Stories

At a boarding school on the coast of Kent my mother
taught a girl who became the Queen of Greece.

She told me this one afternoon while we sewed,
showed me her name in an autograph book,
foreign, girlish and spiky in black ink on a pink page.

As a boy my father had heard of yoked oxen shod like horses
hauling stone gateposts to the highest farm in our village.

He told me this as we stood in the cave of the smithy,
eyes stinging from hot coke fumes, mesmerised
by the chink, chink, beating of hammer on anvil and shoe.

I am not like my brothers, my sister is not like me,
perhaps our parents told each of us different stories.

I have outlived my parents but not their stories,
their stories are mine now to embellish if I wish.

I Am That Child

I am that child creeping through woods imagined wild,
dreaming dangers, rarely fearful, merely waiting,
silent in bluebell-scented air I see sun-splashed
badger cubs play, a twig snaps, they're away!
Old now, I re-enact scenes my memory filed:
the sharp dog fox smell from drooping fern-hidden earth
under larches where at my feet, feathered bones soiled
the clay, and from the shadows his mask glanced rust red.
In moonlight the pale glide of barn owl thrilled,
I heard screech-screeching from the dark hill's trees
where a hidden stone quarry, abandoned, yielded
black waters, wrecked machines and villagers' leavings.
I am that child creeping through woods imagined wild,
dreaming dangers, rarely fearful, merely waiting.

An Obsession with Milk

It begins with the creamy drop
that hangs on the lip of a satisfied baby,
then the white moustache on a child's face
who has drunk from a glass too big for her hands.

Next, she lets a week-old calf lick fingers
dipped into warm frothy milk and shivers
at the feel of its rasping tongue,
eases mouth to pail to teach it to drink, not suck.

Told to watch the churn to catch
the exact moment the cream 'turned' to butter,
she daydreams to the machine's rhythmic beating,
from outside drift scents of hay, silage, muck heaps, cows.

Decades lived away from the farm,
she drives through green lowlands, pastures
where sleek cows put out to spring grass remind her
she knows how their milk will change flavour.

It ends with the creamy drop on the lip
of the frail new grandson who did not thrive.
Cured, he wanted food so much he drank milk
as if he'd crossed a desert to get it.

Daddy

If I had to walk through a room he was in,
I would make myself invisible and slip
from hall to back door, to a kinder place.

He was not like other fathers,
who tickled and sang at birthday parties.
Like an empty building,
he was silent as a wound.

Nothing we could do was right.
When I took him a cup of tea,
I felt relief, reprieved,
if he did not look me in the eye.

Bruno Roughcut, stiff collars, dirty handkerchiefs
and every damned bit of a farmyard will bring him back.
None of the colours I enjoy are his.
Morning skies of apricot and lavender,
evenings of flame and royal purple, they are mine.

To live well now, that is my revenge
on the man who left me cold.
Now, in a kinder place,
I walk with a man who sees me.

Her Secret

One shirt on,
one in the wash,
one in the drawer.
Only ever three, always careful,
never more than you needed.
More would be worse than wasteful,
be getting above yourself,
which was just like showing off.

Then once, in the lull
after ironing was put away, my mother
made us a snack between meals.

From their bed in glistening yellow oil
in a little flat tin with its lid rolled back,
she lifted out and laid on hot buttered toast
cut thin and with no crusts,
slim dark slivers of anchovies—and oh!
the sharply savoury,
deeply fishy,
briny saltiness of them!

This extravagant wonder of a new taste
showed me someone from before my mother,
a life which knew that small luxuries
were an essential need.

Perfect

A pigeon with amber eye and opal neck
swayed and pecked along a littered gutter.
It was perfect, with all its toes
pink and clean scaled, three before, one behind
unlike most of Glasgow's hobbling birds
missing toes and stumps for feet.

When my father left a pigeon for my mother
to pluck, clean and cook,
she cut open its crop, showed it packed
with clover our cows should eat,
as if to justify his shooting
of such softly-feathered pretty things.

At dusk their coo-cu-cooing was a lullaby,
in farmyard and hayloft our constant company.
I wanted that city gutter bird to fly
away from filthy roosts in pigeon ghettoes,
to spend its short sweet life in country living
where it might meet a cleaner killing.

Josephine

Josephine, do you remember me?
I have not forgotten you
standing against the brick wall,
fingers clasped behind you,
teary-eyed, sniffing,
shifting from foot to foot
as if fearing to be hit,

and now I wonder—
did your soft, freckled hands
balling that sodden handkerchief
take impressions,
a sensory memory
of the rough grain and grit of those bricks?

I hope you don't remember
never being picked for a side,
nor joining in our playground games.
If I could meet you now
I would say I'm sorry.

I left the game and stood with you,
not knowing what to say.
Next week you were absent
and never came back.
Did you have a good life?
Do you remember me?

Drifting Apart

At the turning point on our favourite walk—
the children had called it The Loop
when they were young and raced us home—
where it crossed the bed of the stream,
a fox's ribs were scattered like commas.

The skeleton had been washed clean by winter,
yet I didn't see it until I was walking alone,
(three children at school,
husband working away)
when I chose to walk that way quite often,
pausing at the turn to watch its slow dismemberment.

Some summers later we walked The Loop again:
(two reluctant teenagers kicking stones,
the youngest skipping ahead, singing to herself)
and as we crossed the stream I didn't say,
'Once I saw....' because there was nothing left,
and by then we were all drifting apart.

Women's Work

The sombre church of Saint-Sauveur
had an exuberant baldachino,
a Flemish retable and a Madonna, thanked
with votive plaques and candles.
Beyond the nave a woman framed by a door
in a room which was a box of light
was trimming the stems of lilies.
Unaware, absorbed,
she lifted, cut and laid,
lifted, cut and laid;
a living Vermeer.

At the Musée des Beaux Arts,
de la Tour's two women
sat against the dark.
The older raised her hand
in blessing, hiding
the flame which gleamed
on the temple and cheek
of the most real baby in art
in a swaddled cocoon
in the girl's reverent hands.
Rapt, they adored the newborn;
women going about their business.

Still Lives

1

I know a painting of a table draped with a cloth,
its crisp folds, I imagine, put there by a woman
who had scrubbed and wrung the thick stuff,
lifted its weight on to a hedge or line,

folded it firmly under strong forearms,
placed it on a pile scented with sun and air.
On it the artist placed dishes of tin-grey pewter,
brown crocks and a blue and white plate,
on which rest four nacreous oysters
and a cut lemon oozing a drip of sharpness.

Next to the knife which rests on the linen's fold,
there are painted pendants of overripe grapes,
downy peaches and a pair of polished apples;
before the fruit rots the feast will be eaten.

2

I know women who have shelves heavy
with tablecloths they have never used,
embroidered with flowers in featherstitch,
or stiff damask linen patterned with shadows.

These tired cloths, so long invisible,
once brought out on high days for high teas,

laid with bone china and tiered cake stands,
have become an inherited burden,
acquired rust spots of iron mould and
a sorrowful smell of airlessness and dust.

When the women who cannot let them go are gone,
their precious cloths will be found draped
on towel rails which pretend to be mahogany
on stalls purporting to sell antiques.

The Music Lesson

Lady at the Virginals with a Gentleman by Vermeer

She has played a tune in Vermeer's cool air and
her reflected face is as delicate as the painted flowers
on the virginal's case, which the man's resting arm warms.
His singing could flutter the fine hair on her brow and
her swinging skirt might caress the viol on the floor,
when its strings would vibrate with the harmonics of desire.

Believing themselves unique in the history of the world
in their mute passion, they have forgotten the painter's eye,
which maps geometry and makes coloured poetry of light.
The artist pours their hearts into the wine carafe,
collecting in its pale form all they will be
after they have refreshed their dry and smiling mouths.

Pinioned

The gleam of Marsh Marigolds
spilling along the water's edge

caught the sun, drew our walk
to a stone-still nesting swan.

From close by, neck straight out, her mate
lashed the water with determined feet,

made glitter splashes with hurrying wings
to rush a male who dared approach.

Overhead a flying spearhead of swans,
pinions bending the air in unison,
made everything unreal by the bright water,
strange, wonderful, mythical and
brimming with the idea

that Leda welcomed Zeus,
let herself be held
in his wide-arched wings,

to be taken;
his feathered bones
hard between her soft white breasts.

Romantica Beds

In real life you cannot guarantee
Romance will last, nor flower and bloom,
not even, or especially, in a curtained room
for a year for free and five years for a fee.
Promises made in lust and love are meant,
but from birth to death, life has no warranty;
words exchanged as bonds for all eternity
can only be a token of intent.

Though broken things can be mended over time,
both parties know when pledges have expired.
You can't fake love or falsify your dreams,
when unions break they must be set aside, then,
when life and luck bring love again, it seems
already paid for, in pain and baulked desires.

The Beginning of the End

The valley wintry monochrome,
our house below blanket-roofed,
warm lights between curtains.

It had been our only day for it.
Duvets of snow wrapped our ankles,
Larch branches weighted down,
touched, sprang a glitter shower.

Gaining height,
the sky tinted rose,
blue shadows deepened,
afternoon sun declined.
His stride was longer than mine.

Up to my knees stumbling,
sweating, unseeing
uneven ground,
breathing hard.
'Please, let's rest.'
'No, or it will be dark coming down.'
Looked at his stiff back, said
'We shouldn't be doing this.'
His reply, 'You can go back then,'
not a suggestion.

He climbed on,
disdain and snow filling his boots.

My solo descent in the snow was easy,
stepping in my own foot prints.
In the cottage the stove had gone out.

The Wild Atlantic Way

We didn't know it had a name,
so it seemed the signs followed us,
their pert wavy white lines on blue
inadequate to indicate monstrous far-out breakers
heard on wide strands, under always developing skies,
heroic cliffs rising from white foam,
us struggling to stand in the westerlies
that scoffed at summer.

But our road was not all blue and white—
after fields deep-hedged with elderflowers,
verges bright with moon daisies, we had
to come to hard Skibbereen in rain
to hear how once, then as now,
this glorious floribundance
was useless as food, or fodder, how
anyway, all animals eaten,
villages of the dead dragged
into famine pits
dug by skeletons with spades.
The barely alive crawled
to the workhouse
for that last and least dignity,
a coffin burial,
and no help came.

When no help came
survivors looked west,
took ship with their bitterness and rage,

went their wild Atlantic way.
For the rest of our wandering north
we were sore aware, that what's buried
always works its way to the surface,
like stones in a ploughed field.

Sea Meadow

After heavy summer rain
tall meadow grasses
lie in troughs and break into crests,
like a painting of a stormy sea
by Joan Eardley.

She painted on the shore
wind buffeting her boards
sand blowing into the paint
she dragged in swathes
dripped and scumbled,
re-making the sea into a rant
against the tide that takes.

When a rank field under a yellow sky
was her day's obsession,
seeds and stems drifted into the oils
which under her brush
made the wild tangle rear up
from hot compacted earth like a wall
on which she wrote its story.

After the rain a breeze
ripples the sea-meadow,
the grasses wave,
beckoning the end of summer
and the man who comes to scythe.

Seeing and Seeming

The black floor pools away,
laps each column base,
meets aisle walls,
greets east and west,
shuffled and buffed to a satin shine
by compliant feet for centuries.

Every slab is a lid, each lid inscribed
with deep cut emblems softened by time,
heraldic devices, places, dates,
some nameless, all numbered.
The numbers are all awry,
the bones too may lie contrary
to the principles of anatomy.

Light from tall windows glances
off walls the white of cream
making it seem the church lights itself.
A dual colonnade of thick pillars,
intimidating and reassuring
carries walls, arches and vaulting roof,
a ceiling, a cat's cradle of beams
filled in by the boat builders craft,
varnished harmoniously golden with age.

Expectant, generous, reserved,
despite the mass of architecture,
its stories are written in lower case,
in details that need to be read

as patiently as a painting.
Two men and a woman, minimised,
seen far off, stand in shadows
hardly darker in hue than the light,
bringing a moment of doubt;
whether in a picture or the place.

A Sense of Place

From a photo like an image at the edge of memory
paint a sea scene on handmade paper with sable brushes.

The foreground beach must glow with the day's warmth
felt under tender insteps, soles and roughened heels;

translucent shallows reflect blues and colours indescribable
in words, but which float from the brush in pale washes.

To catch the hissing foam and breaking curls of waves
needs care, and you have watched long enough and often

to understand how each current and undertow works, and
where the further ocean needs to shade from teal to cobalt.

Massing clouds above should be backlit by the last of the sun—
let faint shadows fall on the sand to show end of day chill.

It is time to clean your brushes, leave the painting, the shore;
like the ebbing tide, your fugitive colours will fade,

so choose a shell with the meaning of the day in its curves.
It will hold your heart's memory, the true semblance of place.

The Distant Chimney Plume

The distant chimney plume is our barometer.

Horizontal right means chittering easterly,
lazily left it's a walk in the park,
straight up is rare, though sometimes
                                    it all happens in the one day.

That plume in the sky,
grey against white, white against grey,
would pose problems of continuity to an artist.

Monet would have had a go—or four,
Sisley would have liked the dreich days
and although an unlikely choice, Kokoschka
would have given it some welly—and Turner?
                        Well he didn't get to Glasgow

though if he could now
he would paint the contrails
making a Saltire on blue days,
and with a delicate scribble of the finest sable brush,
                would record the distant chimney plume.

The Bay Tree

For five winters it shivered in the sunless cold,
alone in my stone-flagged Yorkshire yard.
A puny bargain, I gave it a home
in a big clay pot, where each year it won through
and sent out bright leaves, viridian when new,
that darkened and dulled until pulled for soups and stews.

It moved with me and lost leaves; waited
until we broke the pot and, with kind words,
spread its roots and firmed the deep new soil.
Now, between warm brick walls, our bay
has become the tree it was meant to be;
sturdy and aromatic among the chives and rosemary.

A Room with a View

Between the treetops and the floor above,
we have more than Cinerama,
we have surround clouds and Technicolour dawns,
private screenings of sunsets that squeeze the eyeballs.

It is a not quite silent film,
our twenty-four-hour movie
with a Universal classification.
Every day's a première of this view of views,
this horizon across which our eyes cannot rest,
this enviable prospect from this room with a view.

With the wider horizon we feel wiser;
as if seeing more, we must know more,
as if now there are no limits
on how you can change your views.

Merely Players

It seems we no longer perform
in the scenes of our children's lives.
We may prop and prompt
but they have grown into their parts,
taken the leads in their own scripts,
so what happened to our roles?

We are allowed to sit in the stalls,
(if we leave the critic at home)
come on as messengers, men at arms,
those nameless ones who
enter, exit, exeunt, noises off,
while our offspring strut their stuff.

But the play in which we star,
have written and are directing,
still runs, with acts and scenes
on, and at, another stage entirely.

Post-natal

On the post-natal ward,
muffled by curtains and caresses,
women's voices floated softly
between bed and cot, lips and breast.
New lives had been set going, new bonds begun.

My daughter's bed was empty.
I dared not look his father in the eye.

In another room
I walked and crooned their baby to sleep,
told him what I needed to hear,
that his mother would be well.
I held my grandson as if by love
I could stop the earth turning.

Now this seven-year old's hair is bright
in the light of the bedside lamp
as he reads, absorbed,
only returning to our world
when his mother
says his name and mine,
then we both say goodnight to him.

Touching

I have so little of hers I can touch:
rings, a gold brooch, a delicate locket.
In the bottom drawer of my desk lies
my mother's album:

marbled grey cardboard covers,
faded black pages,
brittle edges fraying.

Memories of pale hands and gentle face
come back to me through the camera's eye.
Turning the leaves with care
I find my monochrome mother—
young, slender, reclining on the grass and smiling—
perhaps at a father I might have had.

Photo corners grip the small black and white snaps:
people and places that she knew before
life moved her on, before I began.

In pale ink and tiny hand she named them:
 'Langdale', 'Wastwater',
'Picnic Borrowdale',
'White's farm', 'Ambleside',
'Me, June '33'.

Lockdown, Easter

Sometimes, it seems, we could forget—
when stirring a sauce so it didn't curdle,
eating chocolate, listening to Bach—music that
made that shut-in Easter seem safer.

Not minded to believe, absent-mindedly
watching the trees flushing to green,
blackbirds foraging under a braid of briars,
spring as it should be and always had been.

Cold daffodils flirted with the sun and I recalled
my mother who loved their leaves—she picked
them with the flowers for her fluted vase—
and was almost glad she was not there to be afraid.

Sketching you, my pencil paused; you smiled,
then we did forget, for minutes at a time.

I Kept Busy

I kept busy waiting for you today:
shaking and spreading to do the collar first,
then flattening shoulders, smoothing cuffs,
pressing sleeves, lifting over the board,
avoiding buttons on the right front,
ironing the left one and finally the back,
steaming out the creases across the tail.
When I shrugged it on to a hanger
I became that shirt waiting for your arms.

Pompeii

A boy sits on a pavement, bare knees pulled up,
watches lizards flicker between stones and stucco.
It is morning, the sun already hot.
He draws in the dust with a stick, sniffs the air.
Always hungry
he smells hot dough, herbs,
something sulphurous,
rubs his nose on his sleeve.

Entering the square, pedlars of knick-knacks
call to each other in words he does not know,
set out their trinkets.
No-one knows where they sleep.
No-one knows where he sleeps.
The busy city does not care.

A shadow not of the sun moves towards him.
When it reaches his knees he will want to move.
When it reaches his knees he cannot move.
He will always be hungry.
He will always be there.

Iceland

Geological maps show all is in flux,
that plates of the earth's crust
still drift;
that there is a land
where you can stand
where continents still move apart.

That rift is a hundred-mile trench
where the first Icelanders gathered
in their new home, knowing
that nothing was safe—
not homesteads nor villages;
that nothing was sure—
not peaks nor glaciers;
that molten rock
from smoking mountains
might at any moment incinerate their children.
Yet still they stayed.

Tectonic shifts and gross eruptions destroy
and create new lands and mountains.
On fresh charts men give them names,
as if naming can make a thing permanent.

The Island of Rømø

Shrill children flying kites amuse us briefly,
knots of people stand looking out to sea,
cluster round camper vans on the hard sand.
Wind surfers lean and zip
beyond the water's frilled edge.

Suspended in a blue bubble between sky and beach,
we are micro-dots of matter on the endless shore.
With swollen ankles caressed by ripples
making gilt lace of the shallows we stand in,
we wish we could be young again,

or children coming to the sea
for the first time
or the first of humankind
to reach this island,
to feel this small,
to feel this grateful.

Reading Rilke in the Islands

Your gift of his words travelled with us
through a drowned land of rock and lochans
peopled with enigmatic stones.

The wild sea cleansed him with its noise;
at Port 'o Ness foam creamed off cobalt waves.
Rilke told the young poet to be close to things:
'They will not desert you.'

Next day wavelets lapped our ankles,
cast meshes of light on glassy shallows
over hard ribbed and rippled sand.
Clouds draped over the furthest blue Bens
like languid nudes settled on cushions,
boats swung at anchor, prows always to the wind.

A flight of snipe rose as we came, late,
to the dark rocks where sky and sea merged.
It suited us, Rilke's description of love
like two solitudes saluting each other.
Learning your land my beloved, for many nights
our bordering dreams were of islands.

The Buzz of the City

The city's hum is solid,
inescapable.
It cannot be dissected to be understood.

Its billions of constituent parts
are layered molecules of sound
laid down in an acoustic sea.

On the street
the city's hoarse roar
assaults.

It leaks through closed windows
into a room which is silent
but for the turning of a page.

In the park
in high summer,
under the rustling lime tree

dripping with honey-scented flowers,
inside the hive of sound
made by hundreds of bees,

I taste my happiest days
of nearly eighty years
and the buzz of the city is silenced.

To the B6318

The B6318 runs between high fields,
slips past semis and Hadrian's turrets,
by-passes the bus stop at Brocolitia.
To cross the north the old ones trod it first,
then for their legions the Romans paved
a switchback road of straight miles,
with steep bends into wooded clefts—
it's a roller coast-to-coaster ride.
Hadrian's wall is a line in the grass,
long hyphens and short dashes of stone,
forts on escarpments, traces of farms,
Latin words (in brackets) on the map.
A modest name for the edge of empire,
the password for time travellers is B6318.

Time Slip

I was there
saw the plates collide
mountains raised folded
frozen splintered cracked
saw a thick mile of ice laid over the land
glaciers that roared gouged scraped
weighed down plateaux jagged ranges
melted left behind boulders mud rubble hills

saw the land tip and rise again
streams flow from melting ice
become rivers
carve valleys
shape mountains
lichens and mosses drape stones
alder and birch flutter
in meagre soil

heard birds and insects
the first voices in new forests
saw returning eagles circle
deer skitter over screes
when they saw the first men

to walk on the side of Cairngorm
where I imagined I remembered.

Snakeskin

I look at a skin shed by an adder,
seeing what is not there—
the alive-and-slithering-quick snake;
self-flayed, denuded but not naked,
its history left behind, a husk of discarded sensations.

As weightless as the lightest feather,
softly silvered, still coiled,
transparent segments show where belly muscles pulsed.
Pewter-coloured crumpled patterns trace its length.
It has open jaws;
there is no sign of its once-red eye.

In the mirror I touch finger tips to dry cheeks and lips,
seeing what is not there—
the compliant suppleness of youth.
I found a skin sloughed from an adder
and saw there all the selves I have been.

Signs of Ageing

Advert for skin cream: 'Reverses the seven signs of ageing'

The suns of many summers means we are scarred
by long-gone days lazing on shores and grasses.
Our lined and thin-lipped mouths have smiled and laughed,
received and given a thousand kisses.
Joints and skin that no longer stretch with ease
recall limbs entwined and loves' caresses,
but our blood still courses, and we like to tease
the blushing young who prefer us sexless.
We know our flaws, they're friends not enemies,
mirrors show merely what others can see.
This is our best time, telling our stories,
they, not beauty, our immortality.
Seeing us ageing, youth spurns what we've learned:
that what can't be cured should simply be ignored.

And

There were three this year;
the other 'better' halves
taken off.

For years conjoined by 'and'
in address books
now crossed out

to save the shame of seeming
not to have remembered
that this year they've gone,

effaced, ampersand wraiths,
impressions of shared lives
with their still breathing 'ands'.

Still Dancing

She walks her old slow dog, or the old slow dog walks her.
Both sway with flat-footed steps, a funereal march to the Green.
The breeze lifts her hair, the dog raises his nose.
Each sees paths they once paced and raced, vigorously.

When my friend stands, he takes his time, unbends carefully.
In his mind he is flying across a stage to a pulse of unheard music,
telling his life in a language of arms, feet, hands, of the body
in which he has never stopped dancing and dreaming of dancing.

They do not think they are old, not like other people are old.
The lines on their faces are not there when they are alone,
they do not wear them when they are at home.

Acknowledgements

Some of the poems in *Still Dancing* (or earlier versions of them) have appeared in the writer's self-published pamphlets, three of which were shortlisted for the Callum Macdonald Memorial Pamphlet Poetry Prize. 'The Wild Atlantic Way' won the Scottish Association of Writers James Muir Award 2022, and several of the poems have appeared in *Poetry Scotland, The Herald, Gutter* magazine and anthologies published by the Federation of Writers Scotland (FWS).

My husband Raymond is my first and most loving reader; his sharp-eyed comments have helped shaped many of these poems, while his knowledge of my earlier work greatly helped with the selection for this publication.

I have cause to thank those members of The Poetry Fix who offered advice (and support) when it was needed, and friends in The Word Factory. For reading and listening opportunities over the last decade, and for their support for poetry in the city, I am grateful to Glasgow based groups St Mungo's Mirrorball, the FWS, and the Scottish Writers Centre.

Finally my immense gratitude goes to Sheila Wakefield, founding editor of Red Squirrel Press, my editor Elizabeth Rimmer, and to designer and typesetter Gerry Cambridge.

Mary Thomson has lived many lives since she left her Cheshire farm childhood behind at the age of 18. She is now surprised to find herself in her 80th year and in a city flat overlooking Glasgow Green.

One-time art critic of the *Yorkshire Post,* gallery owner, freelance arts writer, essayist and curator (and always a poet), she has read at arts festivals and venues throughout Britain, including at the Ilkley Literature Festival and the Jersey Arts Festival. An equally wide range of commissions from her 17 years in Scotland has included writing poems for Local Vocals dementia friendly choir; Renfrew Burgh Brass Band; Lanarkshire Cecilian Orchestra; Riverside Youth Band; 'Brushes with War, Art from the Front Line' 1914–18 at Kelvingrove Art Gallery; and Bridgeton Library Local History Group's 'Illustrated War News 1914'. In 2018 Composer Nicholas Olsen was commissioned to set her poem 'Singing into Being' to music for the RSNO Junior Chorus.

A NOTE ON THE TYPES

The body text of this book is set in Chronicle,
a contemporary 'Scotch' typeface from the Hoefler
digital type foundry in New York. Its designers
call it a 'hard-working' text face suitable for
a variety of contemporary uses. For historical reasons
Scottish type designers' types, notable for their
functionality and clarity, were widely adopted and
influential in twentieth-century American typography.

Titles are set in Palatino Sans Light, a contemporary addition
to Herman Zapf's classic original serif.